THINGS I'D LOVE YOU TO

Know

ALSO BY D. G. FULFORD

One Memory at a Time:
Inspiration & Advice for Writing Your Family Story

BY D. G. FULFORD WITH PHYLLIS GREENE

Designated Daughter: The Bonus Years with Mom

BY D. G. FULFORD AND BOB GREENE

To Our Children's Children Journal of Family Memories

Notes on the Kitchen Table:
Families Offer Messages of Hope for Generations to Come

To Our Children's Children:
Preserving Family Histories for Generations to Come

THINGS I'D LOVE YOU TO

Know

· A Journal for Mothers and Daughters ·

D. G. Fulford

V
VOICE

HYPERION
NEW YORK

Library of Congress Cataloging-in-Publication Data
Fulford, D. G.
    Things I'd love you to know : a journal for mothers and daughters /
D. G. Fulford.
      p.   cm.
    ISBN: 978-1-4013-2240-3
    1. Mothers and daughters—Miscellanea.   I. Title.
    HQ777.85.F85 2008
    306.874'30846—dc22   2007051370

Hyperion books are available for special promotions, premiums, or corporate
training. For details contact Michael Rentas, Proprietary Markets, Hyperion,
77 West 66th Street, 12th floor, New York, New York 10023, or call 212-456-0133.

Design by Chris Welch

FIRST EDITION

10 9 8 7 6 5 4 3 2 1

THIS JOURNAL IS DEDICATED TO

_____

Contents

Introduction • 1

Us • 3

Details • 37

Remembering • 71

Days of Grace • 93

Changes • 121

Bonus Years • 151

After • 197

For You • 219

About the Author • 225

THINGS I'D LOVE YOU TO

Know

Introduction

Things I'd Love You to Know is a way to celebrate the Bonus Years, the powerful, invaluable time spent between mother and daughter later in life. We are living in an age that longs to remember and connect. Sometimes writing is easier than talking. And writing makes a statement permanent. Each page of this journal shouts tribute and gratitude, and the chance to tell another story.

Small memories define the irreplaceable impact mothers and daughters have on each other's lives. Too often, sweet words of acknowledgment go unsaid. Why? Busy days, mostly. Maybe awkwardness or fear of seeming maudlin or melodramatic. Shyness. Or simply because "It never came up."

There is life-changing value in communication made easy. I cannot count the times I hear daughters say how they wish their mother or grandmother were present to talk about things only she would know. Here you have a chance. Answer questions together or individually, surprise each other, and enjoy. If one prompt or question doesn't appeal to you, skip it! There is no right or wrong way to say things you'd love your mother, or your daughter, to know. And if your mother or daughter is no longer here? Writing doesn't have to stop. Remembering never does.

Things I'd Love You to Know makes it easy to articulate what you hold in your heart.

Us

Us

My name

Your name

Our names for each other

Us

People always say this to me about you

Us

You live . . .

I live . . .

We live where we live because . . .

Us

Every holiday we call . . .

This is what I see when I look in the mirror

Us

I am glad I inherited your . . .

But I could live without your . . .

When you walk into a room I . . .

Us

I worried for you when . . .

Us

I knew you were worried about me when . . .

I wish I could do this as well as you

Us

A phrase you use that I have never understood is . . .

Us

This is what I think it means

I feel I can help you by . . .

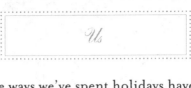

_Us_

Some of the ways we've spent holidays have been . . .

The hardest decision we've made was . . .

We are friends. Could we be roommates?

You drive me crazy when . . .

Us

I know I drive you crazy when . . .

You and I differ in these visible ways

While, inside, we see things . . .

Us

We have lived our faith in this way

Us

You taught me this about friendship

I admire your place in your community because . . .

These are the manners I've learned from you

Us

Our experiences with grief and death have been . . .

We have special words we use with each other

I feel closest to you when . . .

I hear your voice in my voice when I say . . .

Details

Our errands: library, drugstore, grocery . . .

Your desk is . . .

Your stationery is . . .

Your nightstand has these items on it

Your chair and the things around it are . . .

This makes your kitchen *your* kitchen

When we go to lunch we go to . . .

Sometimes you'll snack on . . .

You support these charities

You give your old clothing to . . .

Your favorite shades of lipstick, nail polish,
and hair color are . . .

My laundry procedure is . . .

Your laundry procedure is . . .

The piece of jewelry you can't take off is . . .

The pieces you'd wear to a fancy party are . . .

The best present I ever got from you was . . .

My favorite photograph of the two of us
together is . . .

I want your recipe for . . .

Details

Things I'd find on your calendar are . . .

Things I used to find on your calendar were . . .

Details

We all react to illness in our own way

You love these poems

Details

Your local newspaper is . . .

Your television habits are . . .

Your radio habits are . . .

Your feelings about animals are . . .

Special pets

Cars you have driven

Does your car tend to be clean or messy?

What about your purse?

What about your house?

If you could be anywhere, where would you be?
Who would you be with?

What do you usually dream about
when you dream?

Remembering

I remember you laughing when . . .

I knew why you were crying when . . .

I felt so proud of you when . . .

I loved it when you wore . . .

I did not love it so much when you wore . . .

I used to sit in the backseat and think . . .

I used to look in your dresser drawer and find . . .

I remember listening to you talk on the
phone to these people

Your opinions about my choices in hair
or handbags were . . .

I remember this about you at work

I remember you in these rooms of our house
growing up

I remember you reading books like . . .

And I remember you reading these books to me

My friends always liked you because . . .

Did I embarrass you when . . . ?

Do you remember the television show you called "my show"? The one you never wanted to miss?

I always felt safe when you . . .

I remember we held hands when . . .

I remember your face when you sang . . .

Remembering

Do you remember the time that we . . . ?

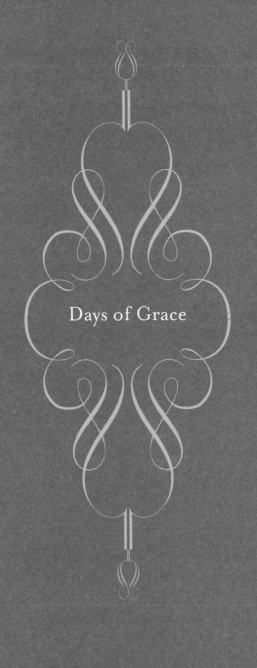

Days of Grace

Your place in the family is . . .

Our circle includes . . .

At gatherings, these people are always present

They are usually wearing . . .

Traditions with this group are . . .

The day I found out I was to become a mother/
grandmother . . .

I felt . . .

You said . . .

The birth . . .

Choosing the name was . . .

Seeing the baby for the first time . . .

Holding the baby, I understood . . .

We've caught sight of these dignitaries and celebrities

We said this about them afterward

I've watched you in the public eye when . . .

And I've seen you in the audience when I . . .

When people see us together they think . . .

When we are together I feel . . .

When you go away I feel . . .

On an airplane you . . .

We like to travel to this place over and over again

You always pack . . .

The room you spend most of your time in now is . . .

The books and music that nourish you are . . .

The food you love is . . .

The look in your eye at weddings
and graduations says . . .

Changes

The look in your eye at funerals says . . .

The changing of the seasons means . . .

Living without a partner is . . .

Each visit with family I see . . .

Friends we have lost

Changes

Who takes care of your outsides?

Who takes care of your insides?

You feel about your doctors . . .

Changes

You feel their nurses and assistants . . .

The soul and the body are . . .

Caretaking feels . . .

Being taken care of feels . . .

Changes

Some favorite prayers of ours

Changes

Some favorite rituals of ours

Changes

We have been through some natural disasters

Changes

We secured ourselves against them by . . .

Changes

When you were sick I . . .

The house ages in its own way

To move or not to move

Packing away and throwing out can be cathartic,
right?

Changes

These are the things we couldn't leave behind

Your infirmities made you feel . . .

Changes

I know you hated to give up doing these things

Your thoughts on canes, walkers, and
wheelchairs are . . .

I understood every woman is bound to be
motherless when . . .

When I focus on the negative . . .

Changes

My ways out of these thoughts are . . .

What are the disadvantages of age?

What are the advantages?

Bonus Years

We are spending our Bonus Years . . .

Some happy surprises the last few years have been . . .

Some not-so-happy surprises have been . . .

You worry about these aspects of your appearance

People say this about the way you look

My inherited traits are . . .

My inherited sayings are . . .

My inherited look is . . .

My inherited stance is . . .

I have felt unable to . . .

Our relationship used to be . . .

Our relationship now is . . .

I knew I was a Designated Daughter when . . .

You thought you needed me because . . .

Bonus Years

I thought I needed you because . . .

Has that changed?

Being a mother and a daughter at the
same time is . . .

I think my life's calling is . . .

Love . . .

And disappointments in love . . .

Some photographs say it all

Bonus Years

I think of you wearing . . .

When I think of you in my mind's eye, I see . . .

You can confide in . . .

We handle a crisis by . . .

These past years have been . . .

I keep noticing things about you
to remember, like . . .

I've learned this about you

And I've learned this from you

I knew I could handle things when . . .

I love the people I love because . . .

Most of the time I feel . . .

The last time I cried was . . .

I am satisfied about . . .

My responsibilities include . . .

My joy comes from . . .

I would like to apologize for . . .

I would like an apology for . . .

My tombstone will read . . .

You chose who you chose to marry because . . .

He chose you because . . .

I know I'll always carry with me . . .

I see the future as . . .

I promise you . . .

After

After

I wish you could see . . .

I wish you could know . . .

_____

_____

_____

_____

_____

_____

_____

_____

_____

_____

_____

_____

_____

_____

_____

_____

_____

_____

_____

_____

_____

Such changes in technology!

After

You gave me . . .

After

I hope I gave you . . .

After

I think I miss you most when . . .

After

You come to me in dreams

You put these songs in my head

I look like . . .

After

I feel like . . .

I consider myself . . .

After

I am grateful for . . .

After

My most current life changes have been . . .

After

Our family has grown in these ways

People and pets in my life are . . .

After

I keep your picture . . .

My work in progress is . . .

I carry you within by . . .

For You

For You

221

ABOUT THE AUTHOR

D. G. Fulford is the bestselling author of several books, including the classic *To Our Children's Children: Preserving Family Histories for Generations to Come,* which she wrote with her brother, Bob Greene. She is also the cofounder of therememberingsite.org, which helps people tell their life stories.

Designated Daughter: The Bonus Years with Mom, the companion to this journal, was written with her mother, Phyllis Greene.

Readers may contact D. G. Fulford at her website:
dgfulfordbooks@aol.com.